icky sticky
readers

Super Sharks

Laaren Brown

SCHOLASTIC INC.
New York   Toronto   London   Auckland
Sydney   Mexico City   New Delhi   Hong Kong

Dear family ^(and friends) of new readers,

Welcome to Icky Sticky Readers, part of the Scholastic Reader program. At Scholastic, we have taken over ninety years' worth of experience with teachers, parents, and children and put it into a program that is designed to match your child's interest and skills. Scholastic Readers are designed to support your child's efforts to learn how to read at every age and every stage.

LEVEL 1 READER
- Beginning Reader
- Preschool–Grade 1
- Sight words
- Words to sound out
- Simple sentences

LEVEL 2 READER
- Developing Reader
- Grades 1–2
- New vocabulary
- Longer sentences

LEVEL 3 READER
- Growing Reader
- Grades 1–3
- Reading for inspiration and information

For ideas about sharing books with your new reader, please visit www.scholastic.com. Enjoy helping your child learn to read and love to read! Happy reading!

WHAT'S A SHARK'S FAVORITE FOOD?

ICKY STICKY STICKERS

Every time you see this sign, look for a sticker to fill the space!

A QUARTER FLOUNDER WITH CHEESE.

Contents

ISBN 978-0-545-87231-7

12 11 10 9 8 7 6 5 4 3 2 1   16 17 18 19 20 21/0

Printed in the U.S.A.   40
First edition, January 2016

Super sharks

There are more than 500 species of shark. Most are small and harmless. YAWN! Do you dare meet... the SUPER sharks? The largest, most fearsome sharks OF ALL TIME? These are superstrong sharks, with super powers and super senses. Come on... take a deep breath... DIVE IN!

⚠ **ICKY STICKY STICKERS**
The great white is the most fearsome shark.

Check out this huge *megalodon*! Millions of years ago, it was the terror of the oceans. Like most sharks today, it was pointy at the front and plumper in the middle. It had a skeleton made of light cartilage. It could cut through water like a torpedo!

human: **6 feet**

AAAGGGHHH! AREN'T YOU EXTINCT?

whale shark: **30 feet**

Megalodon was the largest shark of all time. Imagine a 60-foot torpedo with dozens of sharp teeth swimming after you! Other fish are VERY glad that this shark died out 2.6 million years ago.

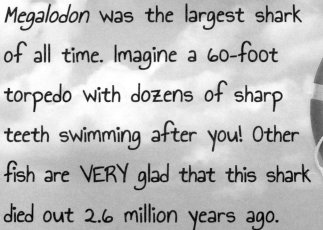

Info bite

New word

cartilage
(say KAHR-tuh-lij)
A strong, flexible material that makes up a shark's skeleton.

megalodon: **60 feet**

DID YOU JUST SAY I STINK?

⚠ **ICKY STICKY STICKERS**

The lanternshark is one of the smallest sharks of all time. It glows in the dark!

Super senses

Super hunters need super senses to catch their prey. A **tiger shark** LOVES the smell of blood. It can sense a single drop from a quarter mile away. It can also sense the vibrations made by fish splashing and thrashing around.

tiger shark

⚠ ICKY STICKY STICKERS

The oceanic whitetip has a super sense of smell—it sniffs the air to find its prey.

It swims toward the vibrations . . . closer . . . closer . . . Hang on! Where are those fish? They're HIDING! Luckily, the pores on its snout help the tiger shark sense the electricity made by the fish. It's dinnertime!

Five shark super senses

SEEING

SENSING ELECTRICITY

SMELLING

HEARING

SENSING VIBRATIONS

Seek and destroy

READY, SET, GO!

When a shark detects dinner, THE CHASE BEGINS! No other shark chases like the speedy **shortfin mako**! This super shark is the fastest in the ocean. It has a pointy nose and a long, slender body to help it slice through the water.

lemon shark:
2 mph

shortfin mako:
31 mph

great white:
25 mph

A powerful tail also helps push the mako forward. The shark is covered with toothlike scales. These create tiny whirlpools, whirrrrrling the shark along, faster and faster. GO, MAKO! Go, go, gooooooooo!

THE WINNER IS . . . THE MAKO!

MAKO MOVES
A mako can jump 20 feet . . .

. . . right out of the water!

11

A **bull shark** isn't as fast as a mako. It doesn't have to be. It's SNEAKY! Unlike other sharks, it can live in salty OR fresh water. It hides in the murky waters of a river, waiting for an unlucky fish or turtle to swim past. And if a wildebeest stops by for a drink and steps out a little too far . . .
the shark may attack!

ICKY STICKY STICKERS

The tasseled wobbegong is another sneaky shark. Its brown body helps it hide on the ocean floor.

WHAT HAPPENS NEXT?

Uh-oh . . . look who's here! A hungry crocodile . . .

. . . and it's SHARK on the menu! This time, our superhero has lost.

Meet one super shark that doesn't need to hide. The **great hammerhead** has a deadly weapon... its HEAD! First, eyes and nostrils at each end of its head help the shark detect a tasty ray.

ICKY STICKY STICKERS

A thresher shark also has a deadly weapon. It uses its tail to whip fish!

14

Next, the chase begins. The wide head works like a plane's wings, lifting the front of the shark as it swims. Then the hunter uses its huge head to pin the ray to the ocean floor. Finally, it BITES OFF the ray's wings. OUCH!

Info bite

New word

ray
(say ray)
A type of fish with a flat body, large fins, and a thin tail.

EEK! QUICK, TURN THE PAGE!

15

Look out! It's a **great white** . . . the most feared shark in the world. This one is really BIG—that tells you that she's female! And she's HUNGRY. Hey, what's that splashing at the surface? A seal? YUMMMM! The shark gets into position below her victim. Then she waits . . . and waits . . . and ZOOM!

SPOT THE DIFFERENCE

To a great white peering up from below, a seal looks very similar to . . .

. . . a surfer! If the shark can't tell the difference, it may take a test bite!

Like a superhero, she leaps out of the water, snatching her prey on the way up. Shaking her powerful head, she rips off bite-size pieces of seal.

⚠ ICKY STICKY STICKERS
A great white pushes its jaw forward when it attacks.

17

Chomp!

Say cheeeeese, **sand tiger shark**! This SUPERSCARY fish swims with its mouth open, showing off dozens of needle-sharp teeth. Like all sharks, it has rows of new teeth waiting to move forward. Sharks grow and lose teeth all the time—some use thousands in a lifetime! Let's meet some other sharks with SUPER teeth!

⚠ ICKY STICKY STICKERS

Many sharks have 40 to 50 teeth in the front rows of their mouths.

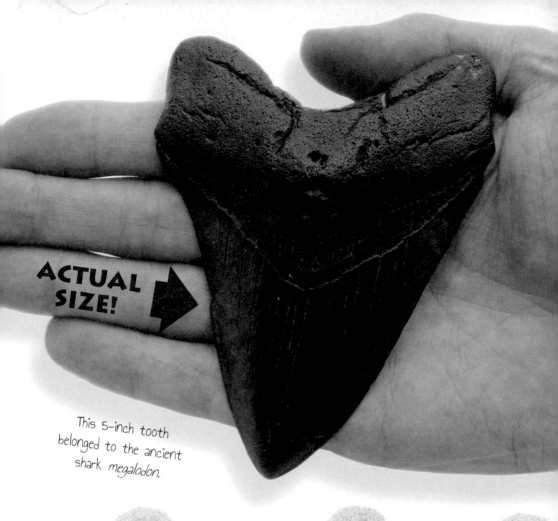

ACTUAL SIZE!

This 5-inch tooth belonged to the ancient shark *megalodon*.

SUPER SHARKS WITH SUPER TEETH

The great white has jagged teeth for sawing through flesh.

The saw shark slashes at prey with its toothy sword!

The nurse shark has teeth that lie flat for crushing shellfish.

Cookie-cutter sharks ... they sound sweet, right? WRONG! Their teeth are NIGHTMARISH! A cookie-cutter stabs its teeth into a large victim, attaching itself with sucking lips. Then it twists to cut out a little chunk of flesh.

Great whites may let their teeth do all the work. They may bite victims and let them bleed to death. It's easier than fighting.

For its size, the cookie-cutter has the largest teeth among all sharks.

ICKY STICKY STICKERS

When its teeth are worn out, the cookie-cutter may swallow the whole row! Then a new row moves up.

Cookie-cutter sharks glow in the dark!

21

Dinnertime!

Think all sharks are vicious killers? THINK AGAIN. The supersize whale shark, the largest shark of all, munches on nothing more than teeny-weeny plankton.

ICKY STICKY STICKERS

⚠ The basking shark, the second-largest shark, also eats plankton.

plankton

This mild-mannered monster can reach up to 40 feet in length. It fuels its massive body by filter feeding. The whale shark sucks seawater into its ENORMOUS mouth, filters out the plankton, and forces the water out through its gills. Every hour, the shark filters enough water to fill a swimming pool!

When it's dinnertime for most sharks, though, plankton is NOT on the menu. Nurse sharks vacuum up crabs and starfish from the ocean floor, while great whites snap up seals at the surface. Small reef sharks hunt fish and squid.

nurse shark

tiger shark

squid and little fish

almost ANYTHING!

The tiger shark doesn't play by the rules. The "trash can of the seas" gobbles up tires, license plates, and shoes! Help these hungry sharks find dinner!

great white shark

reef shark

seals, turtles, and small sharks (YUM!)

I'M ON THE MENU?

crabs, shrimp, and starfish!

25

Deadly dangers

We've met some super sharks, right? And we've met some superSCARY sharks, right? But we almost always have NOTHING to fear. Sharks kill about 5 people each year, but we kill about 100 million sharks each year! We hunt them for food and sport, and we pollute their ocean habitats. It's time to protect our fishy friends—because sharks are SUPER!

ICKY STICKY STICKERS

People in Australia hunt gummy sharks for food. But they are careful not to kill too many sharks.

Sadly, some people eat shark fin soup.

TOP 10 super sharks

Say hello to some record-breaking super sharks! These fearsome fish are the biggest, toughest, strongest, and most ferocious sharks of all!

YOU MAY THINK I'M SMILING. I'M NOT.

1 great white shark

2 tiger shark

ICKY STICKY STICKERS

⚠️ The Greenland shark is a record breaker. It may live more than 200 years!

SHOW-OFF.

3 bull shark

Runners-up

 4 sand tiger shark

 5 blacktip reef shark

6 oceanic whitetip shark

 7 shortfin mako shark

8 blue shark

 9 great hammerhead shark

 10 lemon shark

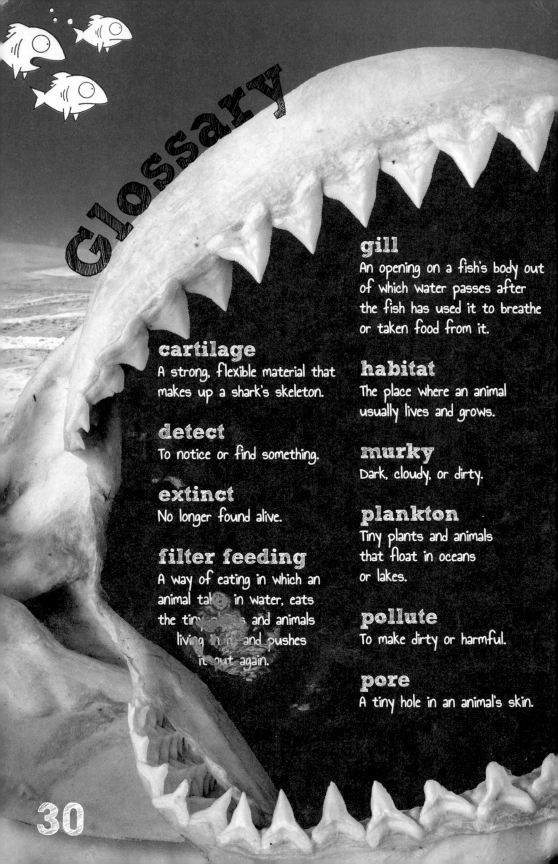

Glossary

cartilage
A strong, flexible material that makes up a shark's skeleton.

detect
To notice or find something.

extinct
No longer found alive.

filter feeding
A way of eating in which an animal takes in water, eats the tiny plants and animals living in it, and pushes it out again.

gill
An opening on a fish's body out of which water passes after the fish has used it to breathe or taken food from it.

habitat
The place where an animal usually lives and grows.

murky
Dark, cloudy, or dirty.

plankton
Tiny plants and animals that float in oceans or lakes.

pollute
To make dirty or harmful.

pore
A tiny hole in an animal's skin.

prey
An animal that is hunted and
eaten by another animal.

ray
A type of fish with a flat body.
It often has large fins like wings
and a thin tail like a whip.

reef
A strip of rock, sand, or coral
just below the surface of a
body of water.

scale
A thin, flat piece of hard skin
on an animal's body.

shellfish
An animal that lives in water
and has a shell or hard outer
covering. Crabs and oysters
are shellfish.

species
A group into which
animals of the same
type are sorted.

vibration
A small, fast movement
back and forth.

whirlpool
A current of water
that moves quickly
in a circle.

Index

Image credits

Alamy Images: sticker sheet gummy shark (ArteSub), 8 main shark (Brandon Cole Marine Photography), 17 main (Dan Callister), sticker sheet sleeper shark (Doug Perrine/Nature Picture Library), 19 bc photo (Marty Snyderman/Stephen Frink Collection), 18 b tg, 19 tg (Tim de Voogt), sticker sheet lantern shark (Wildlife GmbH); Corbis Images/DLILLC/Tim Davis: cover main; Dreamstime: cover cartoon shark, back cover cartoon shark (Dejan Savic), back cover cr (Falkia), back cover tl (FFang), back cover cl (Krzysztof Odziomek), 32 b (Naluphoto), 27 c main (Stefan Pircher), Fotolia: 26 t bg, 27 t bg (Andrey Kuzmin), white painted sign throughout (Brilt), 24 br buckets (Buriy), 14 t main (Falk), sticker sheet shark, 5 br shark (FAUP), 5 bl shark (frantisek hojdysz), sticker sheet thresher shark (Ftlaudgirl), sticker sheet shark, 24 bl shark (Ian Scott), sticker sheet shark, 24 cl shark (Lioneldivepix), 25 bl seal (ornithograph), 29 r bg (orsinico), sticker sheet shark jaw, 30 shark jaw, 31 shark jaw (shizuruvten), 24 bl basket (taviphoto); Getty Images: 13 cr photo, 13 cl photo (Andrew Paice), 12 b bg, 13 b bg (Ben Horton); iStockphoto: 13 tr crocodile, 25 br crate (Achim Prill), 1 main, 3 t fin (adventtr), 8 lightning, 9 lightning (Alek_Koltukov), 9 fish bowl (AlexStar), 25 br snail (arenacreative), 24 bl fish (asbe), 11 cr flag (BanksPhotos), 18 c bg, 19 c bg (Barcin), 4 heart (bobey100), 29 s shark photo (BruceBlock), 10 main, 11 main, 24 7 shark photo (BryanToro), sticker sheet sea urchin, 25 br sea urchin (busypix), 24 br tire (BWFolsom), 24 bl fish (caracterdesign), sticker sheet hammerhead shark, 4 tl shark, 4 bc shark (cdascher), 4 b bg cave, 5 b bg cave (DanSchmitt), 2 c water surface, 3 c water surface, 8 t water surface, 9 t water surface, 32 water surface (Deejpilot), 2 l bg (dejan750), 10 bl fish (digi_guru), 24 br fish (Edward Westmacott), sticker sheet starfish, 25 br starfish (egal), 29 stones (Eivaisla), 3 t sign, 9 wood signs, 9 bl sign (enviromantic), 25 br mussels (eppicphotography), 16 t blood, 17 t blood (freelancebloke), 25 br crate (G-image), 26 br water (Global_Pics), photo borders throughout (hanibaram), 24 cr paper bag (harmpeti), 15 bl reef (haveseen), 24 bg, 25 bg (Haykirdi), 2 bl reef, 14 bl reef (lborisoff), 29 4 shark photo (IPGGutenbergUKLtd), 3 t coast (Ivan Bajic), 9 glass jar (Jiradelta), 9 goldfish (josecauria), 29 8 shark photo (JudiLen), sticker sheet seaweed, 9 bl seaweed, 25 cl seaweed (juniorbeep), 24 br license plate (Kary Nieuwenhuis), 4 c shark (Kitiara65), 24 br oil can (leaf), 24 cl paper bag, 25 tr paper bag (Lise Gagne), sticker sheet tuna, 9 tuna, 25 bl fish (Lunamarina), 4 tr hook, 26 tr hook (malerapaso), sticker sheet coral, 8 bl coral, 25 cl coral (mehmettoriak), 24 br shoe (melkerw), 9 tentacle (mjooo7), 9 music notes (MrsWilkins), sticker sheet whitetip shark, sticker sheet tiger shark, sticker sheet tiger shark, 24 t shark, 28 cl shark, 29 7 shark photo (NaluPhoto), 4 bg water, 5 b bg water (Nastco), 28 bc stones (neamov), 26 br bowl (NickS), 8 b bg stones, 9 b bg stones (nico_blue), 26 b bg, 27 b bg (oilahovik), 25 br seaweed (olias32), 9 eyeballs (OliverChilds), 29 bl squid (PaulCowan), 25 bl turtle (petesphotography), 27 tr skeleton (piahovik), sticker sheet attacking shark, 19 bl photo (Pieter de Pauw), sticker sheet shale shark, 22 main, 23 main (Predrag Vuckovic), sticker sheet shark, 25 c shark (richcarey), 26 br fin (Roberto S Sanchez), 29 9 shark photo (ShaneGross), sticker sheet shark symbiosis, 4 cr shark (stephanik12), 9 red water (sweetandsour), 12 t bg, 13 t bg (tankbmb), 28 br fish (Tarek El Sombati), sticker sheet crab, 25 br crab (Thomas Demarczyk), 9 bg book shelf (ThomasVogel), sticker sheet great white shark, 10 bc shark, 16 cl (Thurston Photo), 16 cr (Turnervisual), sticker sheet lemon shark, 10 cl shark, 29 10 shark photo (uwimages), 2 bl sign (volha), sticker sheet great white shark, 28 cl shark (Vladoskan), 2 r bg, 3 bg, 14 b bg, 15 b bg, 28 bg (Yann Poirier), 21 porthole (yurchuks); Jon Hughes: 4 bl shark, 6 main, 7 bg, 21 t, 21 c, 21 b; Mandy Hague: 11 b shark photos; Museum of New Zealand Te Papa Tongarewa: sticker sheet cookie-cutter shark jaw; Newscom/Andy Murch/VWPics: 5 main shark; Randy Glasbergen: 1 t cartoon, 2 c cartoon, 5 br cartoon, 10 tl cartoon, 11 cr cartoon, 14 cl cartoon, 23 tl cartoon, 27 cr cartoon, 30 tl cartoon, 31 tr cartoon; Science Source: sticker sheet plankton, 23 cr (D.P. Wilson/FLPA), sticker sheet great white shark, 2 r shark, 3 l shark, 28 cr shark (Michael Patrick O'Neill), sticker sheet basking shark (Pascal Kobeh); Seapics.com: 20 bl shark, Shutterstock, Inc.: yellow warning triangle throughout (advent), 14 t bg, 15 t bg (Ethan Daniels), sticker sheet coral, 8 br coral, 25 cl coral (Le Do), sticker sheet diver, sticker sheet eagle ray, 6 diver, 15 b ray, 22 c diver (Mohamed AlQubaisi), sticker sheet tiger shark, 2 cl shark, 18 tl shark (MP cz), sticker sheet hammerhead shark, 14 main shark, 14 br photo (nicolas.voisin44), orange life buoy throughout (Pavel Hlystov), 21 c bg (Rich Carey), 4 bc fish, 7 br coral (Richard Whitcombe), sticker sheet wobbegong shark (Sergey Popov V), 16 blood spots, 26 blood spots, 27 blood spots (yukipon).

SO LONG, SMALL FRY!